Celebrity Bios

MARGOT ROBBIE

Lauren Emily Whalen

WWW.APEXEDITIONS.COM

Copyright © 2025 by Apex Editions, Mendota Heights, MN 55120. All rights reserved. No part of this book may be reproduced or utilized in any form or by any means without written permission from the publisher.

Apex is distributed by North Star Editions:
sales@northstareditions.com | 888-417-0195

Produced for Apex by Red Line Editorial.

Photographs ©: Scott Garfitt/Invision/AP Images, cover, 1; Shutterstock Images, 4–5, 6–7, 8–9, 10–11, 12–13, 14–15, 16–17, 24–25, 30–31, 32–33, 34–35, 38–39, 40–41, 44–45, 46–47, 49, 52–53, 54–55, 56–57, 58; Cameron Spencer/Getty Images Entertainment/Getty Images, 18–19; Hannah Mason/WireImage/Getty Images, 20–21; Paul Zinken/picture-alliance/dpa/AP Images, 22–23; Frederick M. Brown/Getty Images Entertainment/Getty Images, 26–27; Richard Chambury/Invision/AP Images, 28–29; AP Images, 37; John Gaps/AP Images, 42–43; John Salangsang/Invision for the Producers Guild of America/AP Images, 50–51

Library of Congress Control Number: 2023922399

ISBN
979-8-89250-216-0 (hardcover)
979-8-89250-237-5 (paperback)
979-8-89250-277-1 (ebook pdf)
979-8-89250-258-0 (hosted ebook)

Printed in the United States of America
Mankato, MN
082024

NOTE TO PARENTS AND EDUCATORS

Apex books are designed to build literacy skills in striving readers. Exciting, high-interest content attracts and holds readers' attention. The text is carefully leveled to allow students to achieve success quickly.

TABLE OF CONTENTS

Chapter 1

A LIVING DOLL 4

Chapter 2

COUNTRY GIRL TO MOVIE STAR 8

Chapter 3

RISING IN AUSTRALIA 16

Chapter 4

HELLO, HOLLYWOOD 27

In the Spotlight

"IT GIRLS" 36

Chapter 5

HARLEY, TONYA, AND BARBIE 38

In the Spotlight

FABULOUS FEET 48

Chapter 6

BIG SUCCESSES 50

FAST FACTS • 59
COMPREHENSION QUESTIONS • 60
GLOSSARY • 62
TO LEARN MORE • 63
ABOUT THE AUTHOR • 63
INDEX • 64

Chapter 1

A LIVING DOLL

It's a summer day in 2023. Margot Robbie walks the pink carpet. She wears a glamorous outfit. Robbie is promoting her new movie, *Barbie*. Robbie plays Barbie in the film. At every premiere, she dresses like the famous doll. She picks a different Barbie each time.

In London, Margot Robbie dressed as the 1960 "Enchanted Evening" Barbie.

Fans were excited to see which Barbie outfit Robbie wore at every premiere.

In Seoul, South Korea, Robbie is "Day to Night" Barbie. She wears a hot-pink skirt suit and white hat. Then she changes into a party dress. In Los Angeles, California, Robbie is "Solo in the Spotlight" Barbie. Her black gown sparkles. Long gloves go up her arms. She smiles and greets the crowd.

PERFECT FIT

Robbie was first part of *Barbie* as a producer. She wasn't sure if she would act in the movie. But the director, Greta Gerwig, thought Robbie was perfect for the lead role. Gerwig co-wrote the movie's script. She did it with Robbie in mind.

Chapter 2
COUNTRY GIRL TO MOVIE STAR

Margot Elise Robbie was born on July 2, 1990. She grew up in Dalby. That is a small town in Queensland, Australia. It is near the country's east coast.

Lake Broadwater is located just southwest of Dalby.

Margot was raised by her mother. She has two brothers and a sister. As a kid, Margot had a lot of energy. She put on shows in her house. As a teenager, she worked many after-school jobs. She cleaned houses. She made sandwiches at Subway. And she worked at a surf shop.

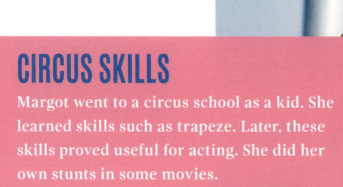

CIRCUS SKILLS

Margot went to a circus school as a kid. She learned skills such as trapeze. Later, these skills proved useful for acting. She did her own stunts in some movies.

Using ropes and harnesses helps people stay safe when learning trapeze.

Margot also took drama classes. She didn't think she would become an actress. But when she was 16, something happened. A movie was filming nearby. The directors asked if she wanted to be in it. Margot said yes. And her life changed forever.

MOVIES COME TO DALBY

Dalby is in a rural part of Australia. Many people there work in mining or farming. But sometimes, movie producers film scenes nearby.

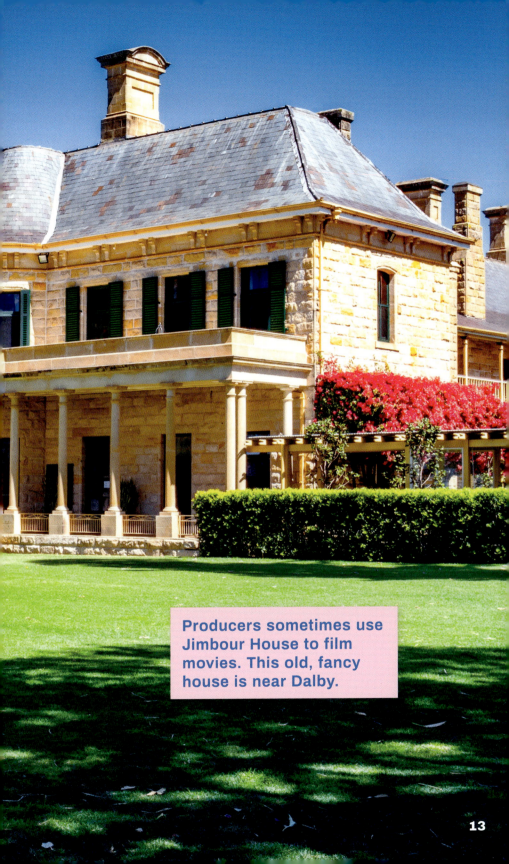

Producers sometimes use Jimbour House to film movies. This old, fancy house is near Dalby.

Margot's first movie came out in 2008. It was called *Vigilante*. The next year, Margot starred in *I.C.U.* This was her first lead role. Margot loved both experiences. She said they were a dream come true.

BUSY HOME, BUSY JOB

Margot's childhood prepared her for acting. Her home was often loud and busy. She learned to be comfortable with chaos. Movie sets can be chaotic. But Margot felt right at home.

Movie sets need many people to control lights, cameras, props, and more.

15

Chapter 3
RISING IN AUSTRALIA

Margot graduated from high school at age 17. She wanted to try for bigger acting jobs. She found an agent. And she moved to Melbourne. She stayed on friends' couches.

Melbourne is a big city in Australia. It is more than 16 hours from Dalby by car.

In Melbourne, Margot started landing roles and attending film events.

Many Australian TV shows are filmed in Melbourne. Margot knew about one show called *Neighbours*. Every day, she called the company that made it. One day, she spoke to a producer. He said they needed a 17-year-old girl. Margot auditioned. She got the part.

COUNTRY TO CITY

Moving to Melbourne was a big change for Margot. The city was much bigger than her hometown. People made fun of Margot's accent. She sounded like she came from the countryside.

On *Neighbours*, Margot played Donna Freedman. Donna liked music and fashion. But she didn't fit in with the other teens. Donna was meant to be a guest character. She would appear in only a few episodes. But Margot's acting impressed the producers. They made Donna a main part of the show.

SOAP OPERAS

Neighbours was a soap opera. Soap operas follow the same characters for years. The plots are dramatic. And the characters are emotional. New episodes air almost every day.

Soap operas need to film many episodes quickly. For *Neighbours*, Margot worked five days a week, 17 hours a day.

Margot Robbie played Donna for almost three years. She also acted on a kids' show. It was called *The Elephant Princess*. But Robbie wanted to act in films. The Australian film industry is small. So, Robbie decided to move to the United States. She thought she could have a bigger career there.

AUSTRALIA TO HOLLYWOOD

Many Australian actors move to America. They often do great American accents. So, some people don't know they are Australian. Famous Australian actors include Hugh Jackman and Cate Blanchett. Chris and Liam Hemsworth are Australian, too.

Liam Hemsworth worked with Robbie on *The Elephant Princess*. He later appeared in US movies such as *The Hunger Games*.

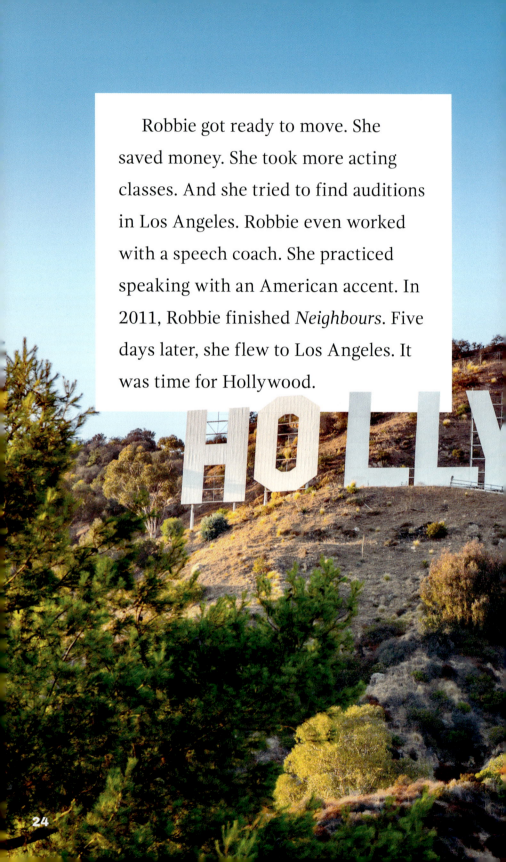

Robbie got ready to move. She saved money. She took more acting classes. And she tried to find auditions in Los Angeles. Robbie even worked with a speech coach. She practiced speaking with an American accent. In 2011, Robbie finished *Neighbours*. Five days later, she flew to Los Angeles. It was time for Hollywood.

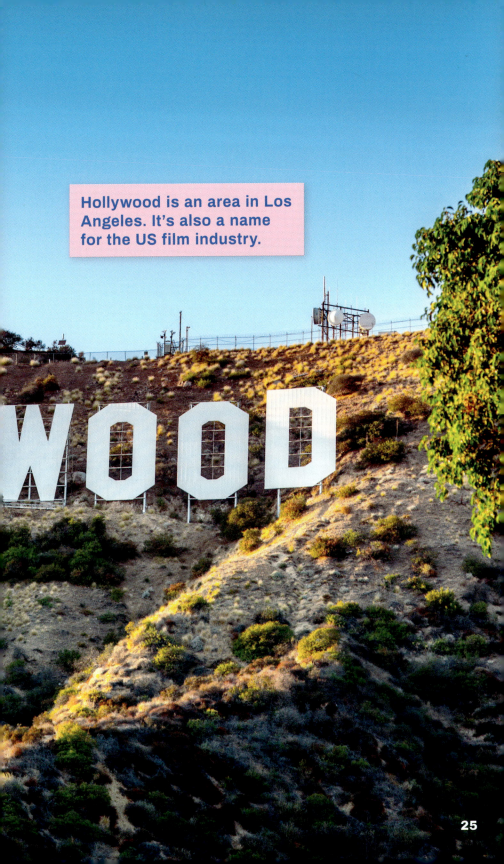

Hollywood is an area in Los Angeles. It's also a name for the US film industry.

Robbie and Karine Vanasse (right) attend a press event for *Pan Am* in 2011.

Chapter 4
HELLO, HOLLYWOOD

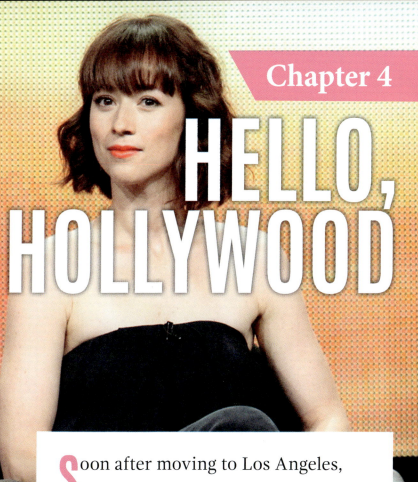

Soon after moving to Los Angeles, Robbie got a new role. She joined the series *Pan Am*. The show was about flight attendants in the 1960s. Robbie played Laura Cameron. Cameron doesn't want to get married. She decides to become a flight attendant instead.

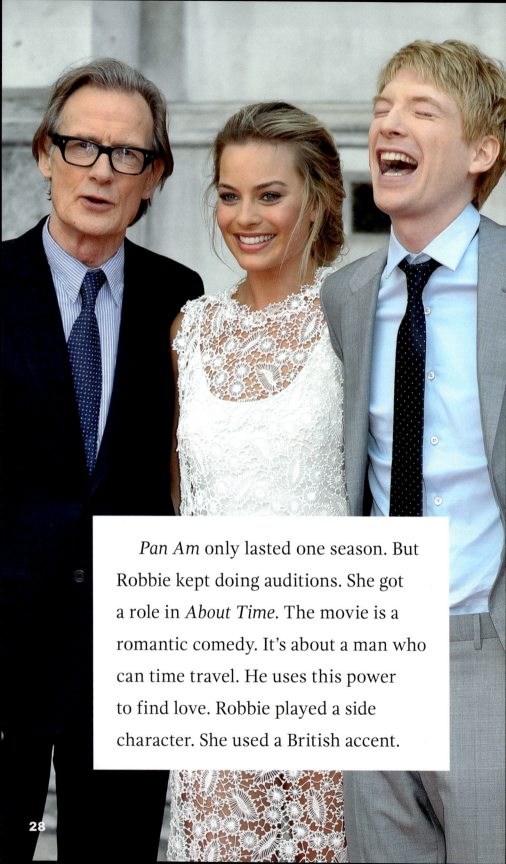

Pan Am only lasted one season. But Robbie kept doing auditions. She got a role in About Time. The movie is a romantic comedy. It's about a man who can time travel. He uses this power to find love. Robbie played a side character. She used a British accent.

28

The cast of *About Time* poses at the London premiere in 2013.

These projects helped Robbie land bigger roles. In the summer of 2012, Robbie's agent called. Director Martin Scorsese wanted to meet Robbie. So did actor Leonardo DiCaprio. Robbie tried out for their movie. It was called *The Wolf of Wall Street*. She got the part of Naomi. Her character and DiCaprio's character were married.

The Wolf of Wall Street tells the story of a stockbroker who committed crimes.

JUST GO WITH IT

During Robbie's audition, Leonardo DiCaprio did something surprising. He started making up lines. So, Robbie did, too. She imagined what Naomi would say. Their characters had a loud argument. Robbie's quick thinking helped her get the part.

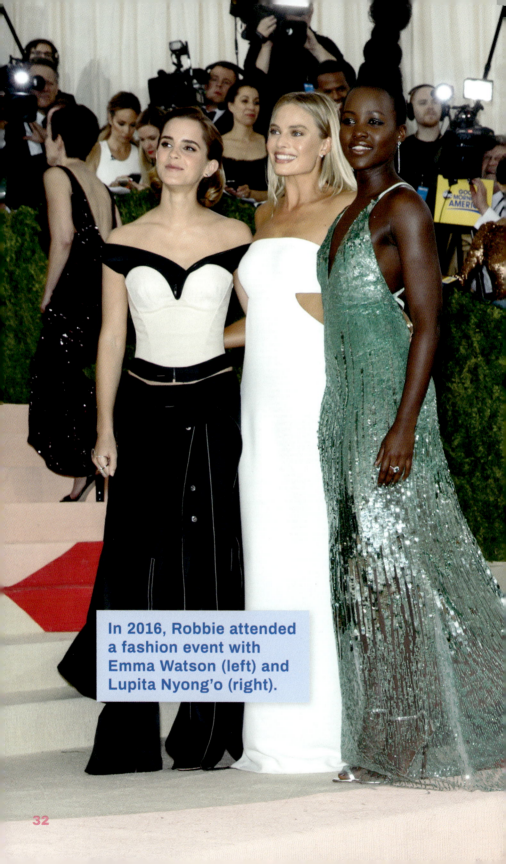

In 2016, Robbie attended a fashion event with Emma Watson (left) and Lupita Nyong'o (right).

The Wolf of Wall Street came out in 2013. It was a huge hit. Over the next few years, Robbie was cast in many movies with big stars. She was Jess in Focus. She played Jane in The Legend of Tarzan. And in 2016, she acted in Whiskey Tango Foxtrot.

STEALING SKILLS

In Focus, Robbie played a thief. She learned pickpocketing for the movie. A performer taught her to steal watches and wallets. That made Robbie's performance more realistic.

33

Robbie acted in smaller movies, too. For example, *Suite Française* came out in 2014. It was a love story set during World War II (1939–1945). While filming, Robbie met Tom Ackerley. He was an assistant director. They got married in 2016.

NOT A MODEL
Robbie has appeared in many big fashion magazines. She poses for pictures. And she talks about the movies she's been in. But Robbie's main focus is acting. She told one magazine that she was not a model.

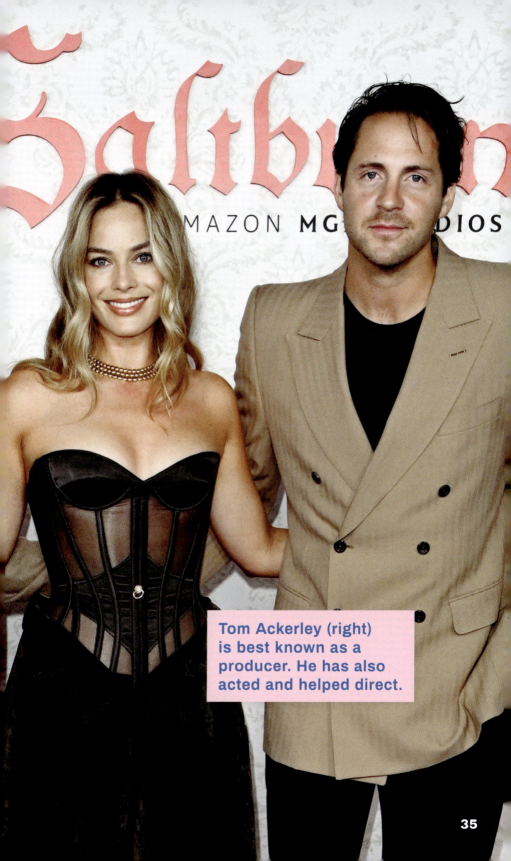

Tom Ackerley (right) is best known as a producer. He has also acted and helped direct.

In the Spotlight
"IT GIRLS"

In 2022, Robbie starred in the movie *Babylon*. She played an actress named Nellie LaRoy. LaRoy was partly based on Clara Bow. Bow was a real-life movie star in the 1920s. She played the lead in a film called *It*. Her character had lots of energy and personality. Audiences loved her. They began calling Bow the "It Girl."

"It Girl" turned into a nickname. People used it for female stars who made a big splash. Robbie's character in *Babylon*, LaRoy, was meant to be like one of these "It Girls." And Robbie became a modern-day "It Girl" herself.

Clara Bow rose to fame in silent movies. She later acted in "talkies," too.

Chapter 5

HARLEY, TONYA, AND BARBIE

As Robbie's career grew, she played many famous characters. In 2016, Robbie joined the movie *Suicide Squad*. The film featured characters from DC Comics. Robbie played Harley Quinn.

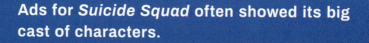

Ads for *Suicide Squad* often showed its big cast of characters.

Fans of Harley Quinn may buy toys or other items based on the character.

People loved Robbie's version of Harley Quinn. Robbie played her in two more movies. One was *Birds of Prey*. In that film, Robbie did more than act. She also worked as a producer.

HARLEY QUINN HISTORY

Harley Quinn first appeared in 1992. She was part of *Batman: The Animated Series*. Harley Quinn is a villain. But she sometimes helps save people. Robbie is the first actress to play the character in a live-action movie.

In 2017, Robbie starred in *I, Tonya*. She also helped produce the movie. It is about Tonya Harding. She was an Olympic figure skater. The film focuses on Harding's rivalry with another skater.

BECOMING TONYA

Robbie looks quite different from Tonya Harding. To play Harding, Robbie wore wigs. She also wore padding on her legs. Harding's strong legs had lots of muscle.

Tonya Harding skated in two Winter Olympic Games. The first was in France in 1992.

In the early 2020s, Robbie helped produce the *Barbie* movie. Many famous actors appeared in it. For example, Ryan Gosling played Ken. Robbie helped pitch ideas for the movie. She worked with the cast and crew. She helped bring the movie to life.

PLAYING WITH BARBIE

Many fans of the *Barbie* movie had the dolls when they were young. Robbie is not sure if she had Barbies as a kid. But her cousin did. The two would play together.

America Ferrera (left), Robbie, and Ryan Gosling (right) attend the premiere of *Barbie* in London.

The *Barbie* movie was a massive success. It broke box office records. It made $162 million in its first weekend. In just a few weeks, the movie made more than $1 billion around the world. People in many countries loved it.

BARBENHEIMER

Barbie came out on the same day as another big movie. *Oppenheimer* was based on a true story. It was about the making of the atomic bomb. Many people went to see both films. People on the internet called the event "Barbenheimer."

Billboards in New York advertised *Barbie*. In some cities, ads were put on buses and cars.

In the Spotlight

FABULOUS FEET

In a preview for the *Barbie* movie, Barbie steps out of her high heels. Even without shoes, her feet stay arched. People loved how this copied the actual doll.

Some movies use doubles for shots like this. The shots don't show actors' faces. So, other people can take their places. These doubles may have special skills or training. But Robbie did the foot scene herself. The shot took eight tries. Robbie had to hold a bar for balance. But she did it. The shot turned out perfect.

The *Barbie* foot shot went viral on social media.

Chapter 6

BIG SUCCESSES

Robbie's work has earned several awards. In 2021, she won a Critics Choice Super Award. Her acting has been nominated for two Academy Awards. The first was for Best Actress. It was for *I, Tonya*. The second was for Best Supporting Actress. It was for *Bombshell*.

Robbie gives a speech at the Producers Guild Awards in 2020.

Robbie worked with Quentin Tarantino for *Once Upon a Time... in Hollywood*. This film first showed at the Cannes Film Festival in 2019.

Robbie has worked with many respected directors. They include Martin Scorsese, Wes Anderson, and Quentin Tarantino. Her work in their films impressed viewers and critics. That led to even more success.

BIG PRAISE

In 2017, *Time* magazine included Robbie in its list of the world's 100 most influential people. Martin Scorsese wrote an article about her. He said that her acting was stunning and powerful.

Robbie helped form LuckyChap Entertainment in 2014. The company wanted to focus on making films about female characters. The characters would have their own exciting stories. Sometimes, Robbie acts in projects from LuckyChap. Other times, she works behind the scenes.

REAL-LIFE STORIES

Robbie often plays complex women. Their stories are not simple. Several of these roles are based on real people. In *Mary Queen of Scots*, she played Queen Elizabeth I. *Once Upon a Time...in Hollywood* is another example. Robbie played actress Sharon Tate.

In *Mary Queen of Scots*, Robbie worked with director Josie Rourke (center) and actress Saoirse Ronan (right).

Robbie's husband and two close friends are part of LuckyChap, too. They sometimes work on movies together. For example, Robbie and Ackerley both produced *Barbie*.

LuckyChap also produces for TV. *Maid* is an example. This TV series is about a young mom. It won many awards. Another show, *Dollface*, showed female friendships. Through both acting and producing, Robbie makes her mark on Hollywood.

Many of LuckyChap's projects, including *Barbie*, have female writers and directors.

FAST FACTS

Full name: Margot Elise Robbie

Birth date: July 2, 1990

Birthplace: Dalby, Queensland, Australia

TIMELINE

1990 — Margot Robbie is born on July 2.

2008–11 — Margot plays her breakout role on the Australian soap opera *Neighbours*.

2011 — Margot Robbie moves from Melbourne, Australia, to Los Angeles, California.

2013 — Robbie stars in Martin Scorsese's film *The Wolf of Wall Street*.

2014 — Robbie co-founds LuckyChap Entertainment.

2016 — Robbie plays Harley Quinn for the first time in *Suicide Squad*.

2018 — Robbie receives her first Academy Award nomination.

2020 — Robbie receives her second Academy Award nomination.

2023 — *Barbie* opens in the United States.

COMPREHENSION QUESTIONS

Write your answers on a separate piece of paper.

1. Write a few sentences describing the main ideas of Chapter 3.

2. What fact about Margot Robbie did you find the most interesting? Why?

3. Which Australian soap opera did Robbie work on for three years?

    A. *Focus*
    B. *Neighbours*
    C. *Birds of Prey*

4. How could working with famous directors help actors build success?

    A. Fewer people could see their work.
    B. More people could see and admire their work.
    C. Other directors could dislike them.

5. What does **complex** mean in this book?

*Robbie often plays **complex** women. Their stories are not simple.*

    A. having no stories
    B. having few parts or layers
    C. having many parts or layers

6. What does **pickpocketing** mean in this book?

*She learned **pickpocketing** for the movie. A performer taught her to steal watches and wallets.*

    A. taking things from others
    B. talking in different accents
    C. trying out for roles

Answer key on page 64.

GLOSSARY

agent
A person who helps an actor get roles.

director
A person who leads the making of a movie.

doubles
People who take actors' places in some scenes. They usually look similar to the actors they replace.

industry
A group of companies that do similar work. For example, the film industry makes and sells movies.

live-action
When characters are played by real people instead of being cartoons.

nominated
Chosen as an option to win an award.

premiere
The first public showing of a movie or play.

producer
A person who helps plan the making of a movie or TV show.

promoting
Bringing attention to something or someone.

rivalry
When two athletes or teams really want to beat one another.

villain
A character who does bad things or goes against the hero.

TO LEARN MORE

BOOKS

Burling, Alexis. *Hollywood*. Minneapolis: Abdo
Publishing, 2020.

Huddleston, Emma. *Scarlett Johansson*. Mendota
Heights, MN: Focus Readers, 2021.

London, Martha. *Chris Hemsworth*. Mendota
Heights, MN: Focus Readers, 2021.

ONLINE RESOURCES

Visit **www.apexeditions.com** to find links and
resources related to this title.

ABOUT THE AUTHOR

Lauren Emily Whalen lives in Chicago with her cat,
Rosaline, and an apartment full of books. She is the
author of several novels, including *Tomorrow and
Tomorrow* and *Take Her Down*, as well as the gift
book *I Heart Jennifer Coolidge: A Celebration of Your
Favorite Pop Culture Icon*.

INDEX

Ackerley, Tom, 34, 56
Australia, 8, 12, 19, 22
awards, 50, 56

Babylon, 36
Barbie, 4, 7, 44, 46, 48, 56
Birds of Prey, 41
Bombshell, 50

Dalby, 8, 12
DiCaprio, Leonardo, 30–31
directors, 7, 12, 30, 34, 53
Dollface, 56

Gerwig, Greta, 7
Gosling, Ryan, 44

Harley Quinn, 38, 41

I, Tonya, 42, 50

Los Angeles, 7, 24, 27
LuckyChap Entertainment, 54, 56

Maid, 56
Melbourne, 16, 19

Neighbours, 19–20, 24

Once Upon a Time...in Hollywood, 54

Pan Am, 27–28

Scorsese, Martin, 30, 53
Suicide Squad, 38

Vigilante, 14

Wolf of Wall Street, The, 30–31, 33

ANSWER KEY:

1. Answers will vary; 2. Answers will vary; 3. B; 4. B; 5. C; 6. A